Praise for *Anxious Little Monsters*

"Anxious Little Monsters takes fear-inducing thoughts and puts them on paper with relatable words and gentle illustrations. It's both practical and inspiring. Great to have on hand in times of need."

—Tim JP Collins, *The Anxiety Podcast*

"What a lovely book this is. Full of helpful sayings, relatable illustrations, and compassion. I loved it."

—James Withey, author of *How to Tell Depression to Piss Off* and *How to Tell Anxiety to Sod Off*

"Simple advice and simple illustration…in the world of overload, that's simply brilliant!"

—Tom Granger, author of *Draw Breath: The Art of Breathing*

"This cute companion guide will help you deal with anxiety and let go of negative feelings."

—Thibaut Meurisse, author of *Master Your Emotions*

"Like having a soothing, understanding friend in your pocket, I want to bring this with me everywhere I go."

—Kate Lucey, author of *Get a Grip, Love*

"These are great little reminders to make us feel better, appreciate ourselves, and stay positive. In fact, they are positive self-affirmations, but presented in a very lighthearted and approachable way. They definitely put a smile on my face and made me feel better personally."

—Niels van Hove, author of the *My Strong Mind* series for children

"I love the way I feel when I spend a moment or two inside Verity's sweet book. These 'Little Monsters' really have a way of becoming 'Little Friends' your mind can hold on to anytime the anxieties of life begins to rise. Highly recommend it for adults and kids alike!"

—Chel Hamilton, host of *Meditation Minis Podcast*

"Verity Crosswell's Anxious Little Monsters are the friends we all need to carry around with us right now."

—Clare Pooley, bestselling author of *The Sober Diaries* and T*he Authenticity Project*

ANXIOUS LITTLE MONSTERS

ANXIOUS LITTLE MONSTERS

A Gentle Mental Health Companion for Anxiety and Stress

VERITY CROSSWELL

CORAL GABLES

For permission requests, please contact the publisher at:
Mango Publishing Group
2850 S Douglas Road, 2nd Floor
Coral Gables, FL 33134 USA
info@mango.bz

For special orders, quantity sales, course adoptions and corporate sales, please email the publisher at sales@mango.bz. For trade and wholesale sales, please contact Ingram Publisher Services at customer.service@ingramcontent.com or +1.800.509.4887.

Anxious Little Monsters: A Gentle Health Companion for Anxiety and Stress

Library of Congress Cataloging-in-Publication number: 2021943451
ISBN: (print)978-1-64250-339-5, (ebook) 978-1-64250-340-1
BISAC category code SEL036000, SELF-HELP / Anxieties & Phobias

Printed in the United States of America

To my family, for all the inspiration and support,
to Rui, for being the best teammate anyone could ask for,
and to anyone who's ever given me a safe space without judging—
it helped more than I can say.

Table of Contents

Welcome

I've had anxiety for as long as I can remember.

At its worst, I was kept up late at night screaming soundlessly into my pillow in pure terror until my body exhausted its supply of adrenaline and I collapsed into a dazed heap. When the alarm went off, I would slap my "mask" back on, ready to go off to school or university and pretend that everything was normal. I didn't even know what it was at the time. I just thought that the obsessive, circular thoughts I got in the midst of a panic attack meant that I was "going crazy"—something which only compounded my fear and made me desperate to hide my symptoms.

Over the past thirty-plus years, I've learned a lot of different strategies for coping with anxiety and depression (the latter being something which, thankfully, hits less often, but still needs management when it does). A massive breakthrough for me was when I met my partner, who suffers from similar issues, and we discovered that a lot of the things we said to ourselves during times of panic or high stress were *substantially more effective when they came from someone else*. Not to mention, it's a lot easier to have a sense of perspective when you're not the one in the throes of anxiety!

With that in mind, I tried writing down some of the phrases we found ourselves repeating the most and putting them on Instagram to see if they might help other people, too. I illustrated them with tiny little monsters going through the same issues—sometimes the monster would be struggling, sometimes it would simply have a friendly face. The cuteness of the monsters makes me want to cuddle them and help them out and, in turn, helps me feel the same way toward myself when I'm struggling.

The AnxiousLittleMonsters Instagram account really took off. I was thrilled at the number of comments I got saying that my illustrations had really helped, or that what I had written was just what they needed to hear at that time.

So I hope it helps you, too. I'm not a doctor or any kind of medical professional—I'm just someone who's found some things to say and do that really help me and others. I would love for them to help you, too.

How to Read This Book

I've arranged the chapters in this book like a journey, starting when you're in a crisis and ending with finally seeing a way out. My idea was to have you start from the point you're at—whether that's in a full-blown panic attack, feeling guilty that you've had one, accepting that life is sometimes challenging, or simply needing a little encouragement to go do the things. Once you've read that chapter, the most helpful for you will then be the following one.

But you don't have to read this book that way at all! You can jump in and out, skip chapters, read it backwards… whatever works for you.

I had to pick a way to organise it though, so here it is.

False alarm: for when your anxiety is in overdrive, you're having a panic attack, or you're full of worries that won't go away.

Mud-tinted glasses: for when your brain is telling you that absolutely everything is awful, you feel weighed down by life, or everything seems very bleak.

Cut yourself some slack: When you're feeling bad about yourself for how well you're (not) keeping up with life, for the things you struggle with that others don't seem to, or for even having a mental illness at all.

It's okay to be little: When you're completely overwhelmed, and even looking after yourself feels like an insurmountable task, read this chapter to remind yourself it's okay to be little.

Look after yourself: We all need to take care of ourselves but it's easy to forget or deprioritise. Here are some gentle self-care reminders to help you on your way.

Sometimes life sucks: Sometimes things really do. just. suck. Things are hard, whether internally or externally, and there's not a lot you can do to change it. The monsters in this chapter are going through it with you and they'll be there every step of the way.

Bright times ahead: Sucky as it might be, it WILL pass, and it DOES pass. Read this chapter when you need some gentle optimism that the sun will shine again in the future.

You got this: Ready to go but need a little push? This chapter is for when you're being brave and doing scary things (who cares whether they're scary to someone else?) and need some gentle encouragement to be your best you.

CHAPTER 1

False Alarm

Anxiety is horrible. I've struggled with it for a long time. And I know that, more often than not, fighting any kind of panic only makes it worse. If you can manage to accept it as something that is terrifying but will recede—like a storm—it's an awful lot easier to not get swept away by it.

One of the things that helps me with acceptance is to think of an anxiety or panic attack as a false alarm. My body and brain's reactions aren't wrong or bad—they're trying to keep me safe by sending out an alert! The part that's gone wrong is that they've been falsely triggered by something that isn't dangerous. Kind of like when the smoke alarm goes off when you've burnt the toast! It's not exactly pleasant when it happens, but you wouldn't want to go without a smoke alarm. And once you've worked out that it's being triggered by the toast and not a kitchen fire, you know that you don't have to evacuate the building.

your body is reacting to a threat

this is perfectly normal

it's just a false alarm

you can get
through this

you don't need
to fight these
feelings

they will pass

it's not your fault
your brain is
lying to you

the panic will pass
and you will remain

You aren't being
sensitive or dramatic.
You're hurting
and that's okay.

These feelings
are scary
but you are not
in danger

you're having some
scary thoughts
right now

but it's just panic

it will pass

focus on your breathing

sometimes
our thoughts
mislead us

It's not all going wrong.

One or two things have gone
wrong and your anxiety
overreacted.

the storm feels terrifying when
you're caught in it

but it passes

it always passes

the world is actually
a much better place
than it seems like

through
your
anxiety-tinted
glasses

you are allowed to feel
what you're feeling

That little voice telling you
you're doing it all wrong?

It's just your anxiety.

It's not true.

your feelings are
not always rational

you're going
to be okay

CHAPTER 2

Mud-Tinted Glasses

Depression—whether it's seasonal, situational or chronic—can really distort your view of the world. Even if you haven't been diagnosed with depression, a persistent low mood can really mess with your brain. Seeing the world through "rose-tinted glasses" is when your perspective is colourful, warm, and enchanted. Depression or low mood is like the opposite—you view everything as darker and murkier than it really is, as if your glasses are smeared with muddy water.

Like the anxiety chapter, the monsters here are not about fixing or curing your low mood, but about taking a step back and realising that perhaps you might not be interpreting things very accurately right now. Even if you still feel the same, knowing that the things you're telling yourself might not be true after all can offer a tiny light in a very dark room.

Your thoughts are just thoughts.

They may not be true.

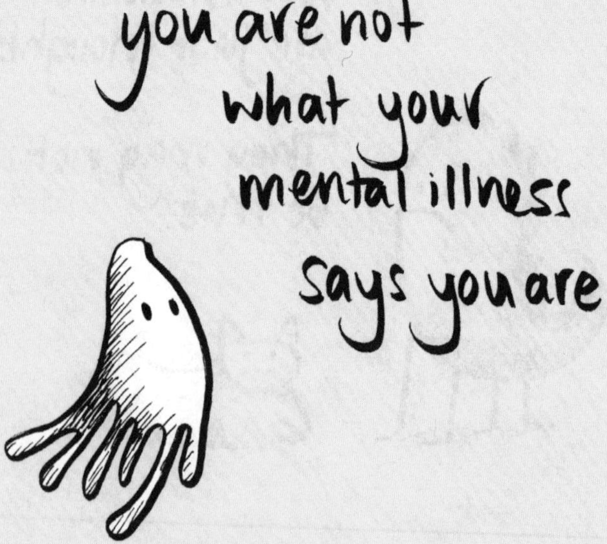

you are not
what your
mental illness
says you are

it's just a thought.
focus on your senses.

don't let
it spiral.

don't believe the things
you tell yourself
when you're sad and alone

you are not a burden

you are a human

depression

lies

your thoughts
are <u>not</u> facts

but your
feelings
<u>are</u> valid

you don't have to pretend
to be okay

depression doesn't make you inferior

that's just what it wants you to think

jus admitting
you're not okay
is a HUGE
first step

you've had good days before.

you will have them again.

please keep going

people care about you.

even the ones who don't
always understand.

when we are
unwell

we
can't
always
see
clearly

CHAPTER 3

Cut Yourself Some Slack

As if dealing with mental ill health wasn't bad enough, we often have to deal with feeling guilty about having a mental illness on top of that. It's a vicious cycle.

When you look around and compare yourself to everyone else, it's easy to feel less than. But someone struggling up a hill with a huge boulder on their back is not doing a worse job than someone springing lightly up the hill who is not carrying that same boulder. Mental illness makes things *hard*. Give yourself some credit for continuing with all you have to deal with!

you are stronger
than you
think

just look at what
you have to
deal with!

having a mental
illness doesn't make
you lazy

in fact, it makes you
great at overcoming
      complex challenges

it's okay to
be a
work in
progress

you are you ♡

you are allowed
to be sad

your mental illness
doesn't define you

just because you had
a bad day
doesn't mean you're not
handling things.

everyone gets bad days.

you will never
be perfect.

no one is.

you don't have to
hide who you are

none of your scars
make you any less
worthy or loveable

you're not broken or wrong.

everyone's brain is different.

Don't let people
shame you for
not feeling happier

You're just having
a bad day.

This isn't
who you are.

Just because
today sucks
doesn't mean
you suck

we can only
move forwards

just because your
path is different

doesn't mean you
are lost

mistakes are part of life

what you did
accomplish
is just as important
as what
you didn't

one day at a time

look at all you've
been through
and you're still here

I am so so proud of you
for the effort you put in
just to keep going

NOBODY does
everything right

everyone's a little bit
broken

it's not just you

you are fighting battles
that some people can't
even imagine

every day

you did the best you could
with the knowledge you had
and the person you were
at the time

CHAPTER 4

It's Okay to be Little

Sometimes you might feel great. You're coping and able to push out of your comfort zone and get on with all those tasks you've been putting off.

But sometimes the world feels overwhelming and you just want to curl up under the duvet and hide.

That's natural—life is made of cycles of comfort and growth. It's not good to stay in your comfort zone *all* the time, but sometimes comfort is exactly what you need. It can be easy to forget that.

If you're feeling little, that's your body's way of protecting itself— so let yourself be little for a bit. If it helps, try thinking of yourself as a scared child and comfort yourself with blankets, hugs, and anything else that feels right.

We'll get to self-care actions in the next chapter. For now, let yourself be small. Don't fight it. This is what your body and mind are telling you they need. And it's *okay*.

the world needs
soft as well as
tough

it's okay to have
bad days

they will
pass

do what you need
to do to look after
yourself

If you need to hide
from the world
for a while

that's
okay

you don't have
to be big
all the time

it's okay to ask for help

You are still worthy
of love even if you
accomplished
absolutely
NOTHING
today.

a rest is not defeat

when life is overwhelming
   it's important to have
some time and space
    where you don't
       have to do anything

do what you need to
to get through the day

It's okay to have
a good cry

it's okay to stay
in your comfort zone
sometimes too

you have been so
brave lately

you can have a
rest now

there is
space
for you
here

the things you found
comforting as a child

might bring you comfort
as a grown-up too

it's okay to take
a break

you can only
do your best

go at your own pace

find something squishy

and hug it right now

It's okay not to do
all the things.

this is where
you are today

and that's
okay

it's okay to be lost
for a while

you can find
your way
later

not everything
that weighs
you down

is yours
to carry

hiding under a rock
isn't always bad

sometimes it's what
you need to do

to grow stronger

and emerge to
crush your enemies

CHAPTER 5

Look After Yourself

Hey you.

Yes, you.

Have you let yourself get a bit run down and overwhelmed? That's okay—we all do it. (I can't count the number of times I did it while working on this book!)

It's time to look after yourself now, though. Let these monsters and your own actions remind you that yes, you do deserve to be looked after. Even if you don't fully believe it now, making the choice to spend time looking after yourself can bring you a baby step closer to a place where you can one day believe it.

If you need ideas, start small. You could do something as simple as brushing your teeth, drinking a glass of water, or going outside to get some fresh air and daylight. Even just slowing down and actually acknowledging your feelings can count as looking after yourself.

If you find yourself struggling to justify spending time on yourself in this way, especially if you're someone who spends a lot of time looking after others, consider this: you will be substantially more effective at looking after others if you've looked after yourself first. As the saying goes, you can't pour from an empty cup, and when your own cup is full, you'll find it so much easier to fill others' without snapping, grumping, or just plain running out of steam.

this is your
official permission
to take care
of yourself

listen to
your needs

you deserve
to rest

schedule in some
time to NOT be
productive

how you feel
matters

slow down

give yourself time
to play

you don't have to do
all the things

self-care
isn't selfish

put your own
oxygen mask
on first

make some space

to just be

make sure
you get enough
daylight

do something nice
for yourself

right now

be with the people
who make you smile

you don't need to do everything all at once

this is just to remind you
that "doing your best"
doesn't mean pushing
yourself to the point
of a mental breakdown

do what you can

accept
"good enough"

Don't forget to look after yourself today

notice life

get some
fresh air

you deserve
nice things

you have been pushing
and pushing but now
it's time to stop and
take care of yourself

you need this

CHAPTER 6

Sometimes Life Just Sucks

Sometimes life really does suck, and no amount of "oh well never mind" or "look on the bright side" is going to change that.

Misfortune, pain, loss, and mental distress are all parts of life. Real parts of life.

It's okay to scream.

It's okay to cry.

It's okay to be sad, or angry, or hopelessly lost. It's even okay to be happy—it doesn't invalidate the rest of your struggle or make you a bad person.

Everybody goes through really tough times. It's okay to admit that and acknowledge that this is really crap. You might find yourself overwhelmingly sad or angry at what life has dealt you. Don't feel like you can't give in to that. It's part of coping. You can move on later when you're ready.

In the meantime, these monsters are here with you. I'm here with you.

And yes, this really sucks.

it really sucks that
you have to deal with
this right now

sometimes you've
just got to muddle
along in whatever
way you can

You're allowed to be

angry

this has
happened
to you.

it's okay
to not be okay

don't give up.

you've made it
   this far.

it's okay to feel
a bit rubbish
sometimes

it's okay to hurt

don't hold back
your tears

healing is
a process

sometimes life just sucks

you don't have
to smile
if you don't
want to

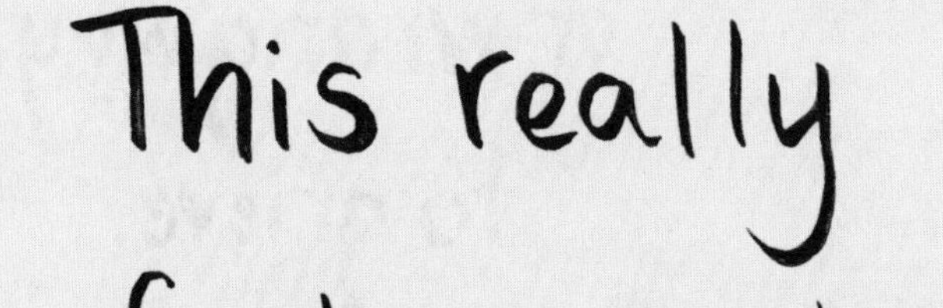
This really
f king sucks

There is no right
or wrong way
to grieve.

everyone's mountains are different

it won't be
the same

but it will
be okay

some days
are just
bad days

baby steps

You're playing life
on extra hard mode
right now

Cut yourself
some slack

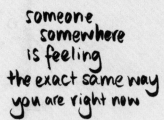

someone
  somewhere
 is feeling
the exact same way
 you are right now

you are allowed
to grieve what
might have been

You're not alone.
There are people
who care about
you.

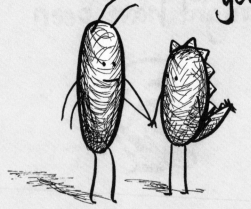

reach out

It is horrible that you have to go through this.

I think you are an amazing human being doing your best with some really hard human things right now

you are doing
hard things

hard things
are hard!

CHAPTER 7

The Sun Will Return

When you're in the middle of things, whether they're external (job loss, exam stress, bereavement) or internal (panic attack, bout of depression), it's hard to believe things will ever be any different. And glib reminders can sometimes seem like they're minimising the pain.

But the thing is, *everything* changes. *Everything* passes. Even though what you're feeling seems like it will never end, the sun will return. Maybe not as brightly, maybe not as dramatically—or maybe even brighter than before. You won't know until you get there.

Knowing it will get better doesn't change how you're feeling right now, and it doesn't change the situation you're dealing with, whatever that may be. But keep that knowledge in the back of your mind. This might be unbearable, but it isn't how it always will be.

hang in there

you've handled
worse than this

whatever happens
we can figure out
a way to make it okay

remember all those
other times you thought
you wouldn't make it
through?

you did, though.

and you'll make it
through this too.

storms
don't
last
forever

everything will
be okay

recovery
is
lifelong

some things you
don't get over

but you do get through

you won't always feel like this

you will feel
normal again

It will all work out
somehow.

It usually does

scars tell your
past
not your future

You've done this before.

You can do this again.

Tomorrow is another day

you will get
through this

better things
are coming

you are safe

you are loved

everything is going
to be okay

CHAPTER 8

You Got This

Sometimes you feel big. Sometimes you feel small. Sometimes you feel just a little bit braver than yesterday, able to reach forward and take the next step.

If you're reading this, it's likely that you're thinking of taking some step or another. It's okay if you're not feeling very brave! The very fact that it seems scary to you means you're being brave just by doing it. Don't forget, you can still do things when you're anxious.

You've dealt with so much so far—some things which might seem tiny now but were huge at the time, and other things that you still struggle with but you've done nevertheless. You've wondered before how you'll ever get through, but you did it.

You'll manage this, too.

After all, you got this far, didn't you?

I believe in you

you got this far

things usually go better than you think they will

it's normal to be
nervous
about new things

just because
you're scared
doesn't mean
you can't do it

remember
how far you
have come

celebrate the small wins

You are resilient
and capable.

You will
survive
this.

Tomorrow will be better

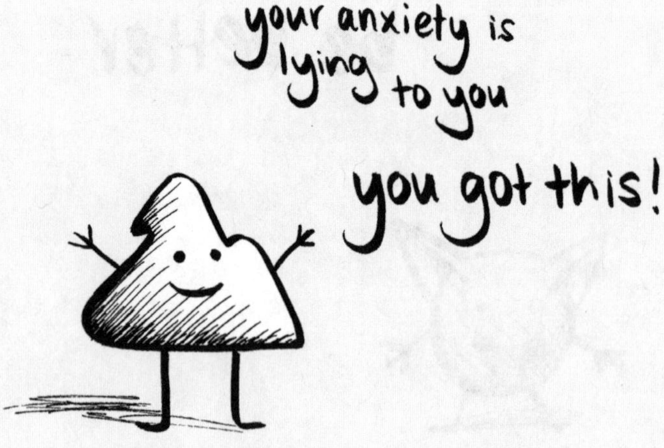
your anxiety is lying to you
you got this!

you are strong

(even when
you feel
weak)

one step
at a time

look at all the things
you've dealt with
so far

you can still do things
even when you're anxious

it gets better
from here

Conclusion

It's hard to write an ending to a book like this because mental health doesn't really have an end point. Anxiety is a mental illness, but it's also an emotion, so you'll never be completely free of it. And sometimes, just as you feel like you've recovered from one setback, life hits you with something else. Things keep moving forward, for better or worse, and all any of us can really do is muddle along.

With that said, a lot of life is about managing your emotional responses to things. If you're anything like me, you'll tend to extrapolate your current mood into the future as if that's how you're going to feel forever. That's lovely when you're feeling happy or successful of course, but it's not so helpful when you're feeling something more negative!

Something that really helps me at times like this is **getting a change of scene, some fresh air**, and, if possible, **getting out into nature**—all three if I can! But if I can't do all three, then just opening a window (fresh air) or going to the next room (change of scene) still helps. Fresh air and a change of scene can help stir my brain out of the stupor that it's in, and getting out into nature helps remind me that I'm part of something bigger. The passing of the seasons reminds me that everything moves on. Nature has its cycles and so do people. Even if I'm going through a whole string of bad days or weeks, they will eventually pass. My job in the moment is to just look after myself as best I can.

Another super helpful thing is **looking after my body**. I'm talking about the real basics here. I always feel better after showering, or putting on clean clothes, or changing the sheets. The same goes for feeding myself something nourishing or brushing my teeth. It's easy to not bother taking care of yourself when you're feeling crappy, but slouching around feeling grubby or grimy really doesn't help your mood, and a few tiny steps can make you feel better. Don't feel like you have to do the whole lot if that sounds exhausting. Even if you just give yourself a good old wipe with a baby wipe (search "antibacterial body wipes" for some really effective ones) and put on new deodorant, it can give your brain a little shift.

I also try to **not fight the mood I'm having**. I've brought this up a few times throughout the book, but it's so important that I'm mentioning it again here. When I'm panicking, my initial emotional response is usually to either panic more ("Nooooo, not a panic attack, I don't want a panic attack now!") or try and fight it with logic, neither of which are helpful and both of which tend to make it worse. But I know I'm halfway to calming down already when I can remember to think: "Ahh yes, this is a panic attack. God, this feels awful. But it's just a false alarm and it will go away again if I just wait it out." And it takes practice to remember! Don't beat yourself up if you're not very good at it at first!

Another helpful activity is **creating**. There are a few different ways that creative tasks help me. Drawing Anxious Little Monsters helps remind me of what's important and helps me create affirmations that I can turn to in darker moments. Sharing those drawings helps me connect with others online and makes me feel like I'm putting some good back into the world.

There's another category of creative outlets that helps me in a different way: activities that are quite repetitive, that need concentration but not very much decision making, like crochet, macramé, or Zentangle. These help to take me out of my own mind. I don't need to think very much, but the concentration helps keep me from getting lost in thought spirals or overthinking. In particular, these are a great for unwinding after a period of emotional or mental exhaustion.

Finally, creative projects can be an emotional outlet in themselves. Feelings need somewhere to go, and an emotional drawing, or painting, or even just a load of words scribbled on a piece of paper can help me get things out of my head, giving myself a bit more room to breathe in there.

I really hope that the reminders in **this book** have helped you, and that they will continue to help you for a long time to come. Feel free to **come back to it again** and again whenever you need to.

Remember, you don't need to be able to do the whole journey all in one go. Just take the next step.

Good luck on your journey. I'm rooting for you.

You got this.

P.S.

I really hope this book helped you. It's the first one I've ever written, and I'd love to connect with you on Instagram or Twitter and hear which parts you particularly liked. If you'd like to keep up with anything else I write or create, pop on over to anxiouslittlemonsters.com/newsletter to sign up for updates.

Now, I've had it drummed into my head that reviews can make or break a book, so if you liked it, please give it a positive review and tell your friends about it (or buy them a copy!). If you didn't like it, well, you know what they say you should do if you can't say anything nice…!

Thanks for reading :)

About the Author

Verity Crosswell is an author, illustrator, and excitable human being muddling her way through life. Her cute and comforting illustrations provide gentle reminders that help with life's challenges without minimising struggles. She grew up in southern England but has now made Edinburgh her home—hail and all. When she's not drawing, painting, or manning her online store, you can often find her in her local cat café.

You can buy prints and gifts of her illustrations from her Etsy store, Anxious Little Things, or come and say hi on Twitter or Instagram. *Anxious Little Monsters* is her first book.

Twitter: @anxlilmonsters
Instagram: @anxiouslittlemonsters
Website: anxiouslittlemonsters.com
Etsy store: @AnxiousLittleThings

Mango Publishing, established in 2014, publishes an eclectic list of books by diverse authors—both new and established voices—on topics ranging from business, personal growth, women's empowerment, LGBTQ studies, health, and spirituality to history, popular culture, time management, decluttering, lifestyle, mental wellness, aging, and sustainable living. We were named 2019 and 2020's #1 fastest-growing independent publisher by *Publishers Weekly*. Our success is driven by our main goal, which is to publish high-quality books that will entertain readers as well as make a positive difference in their lives.

Our readers are our most important resource; we value your input, suggestions, and ideas. We'd love to hear from you—after all, we are publishing books for you!

Please stay in touch with us and follow us at:

Facebook: Mango Publishing
Twitter: @MangoPublishing
Instagram: @MangoPublishing
LinkedIn: Mango Publishing
Pinterest: Mango Publishing
Newsletter: mangopublishinggroup.com/newsletter

Join us on Mango's journey to reinvent publishing, one book at a time.